COMPOSER SHOWCASE
HAL LEONARD STUDENT PIANO LIBRARY

T0081598

Mini OVERTURES

16 FAMILIAR TUNES FOR A YOUNG PIANIST
ARRANGED BY DENNIS ALEXANDER

ISBN 978-1-70513-705-5

HAL•LEONARD®

Visit Hal Leonard Online at
www.halleonard.com

Contact us:
Hal Leonard
7777 West Bluemound Road
Milwaukee, WI 53213
Email: info@halleonard.com

In Europe, contact:
Hal Leonard Europe Limited
42 Wigmore Street
Marylebone, London, W1U 2RN
Email: info@halleonardeurope.com

In Australia, contact:
Hal Leonard Australia Pty. Ltd.
4 Lentara Court
Cheltenham, Victoria, 3192 Australia
Email: info@halleonard.com.au

Preface

I have found that children around the world universally love the music of folk songs, as well as the many nursery rhymes, rounds, and happy tunes like "Eensy Weency Spider" or "The Wheels on the Bus." This collection is intended to provide excellent reading material for the young pianist during their first months at the piano, and the optional accompaniments should motivate them to play with even more character and rhythmical understanding.

This introductory collection is the perfect supplement for any beginning piano method. Most of the pieces consist of single-line melodies divided between the hands, while gradually introducing hands together playing in its simplest form. The words for each piece are included, and students and teachers are encouraged to sing these delightful tunes while performing them! The lyrics help young pianists to shape musical phrases, understand the character and style, and will undoubtedly elicit some laughter or giggles from time to time.

Dennis Alexander
July 2021

Contents

One, Two, Three, Four

Traditional Nursery Rhyme
Arranged by Dennis Alexander

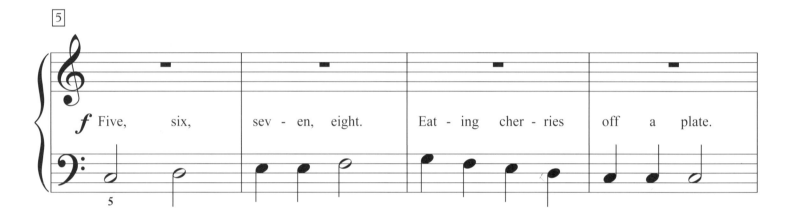

Optional Accompaniment (Student plays one octave higher than written.)

Little Miss Muffet

Traditional
Arranged by Dennis Alexander

Optional Accompaniment (Student plays one octave higher than written.)

London Bridge

Traditional
Arranged by Dennis Alexander

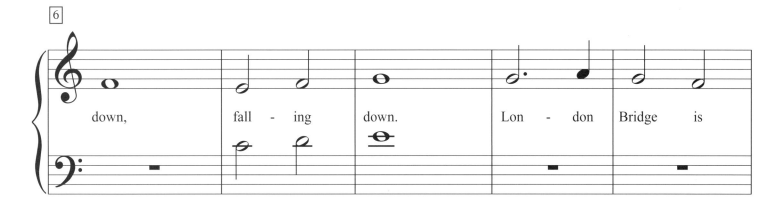

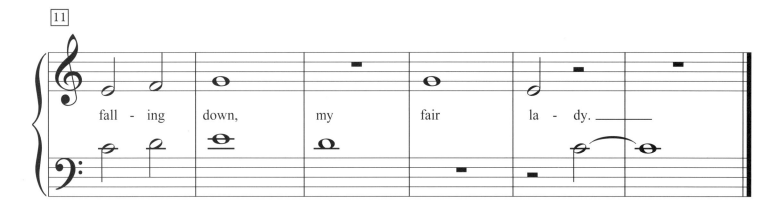

Optional Accompaniment (Student plays one octave higher than written.)

Very quickly (♩ = 196–200)

Twinkle, Twinkle, Little Star

Traditional
Arranged by Dennis Alexander

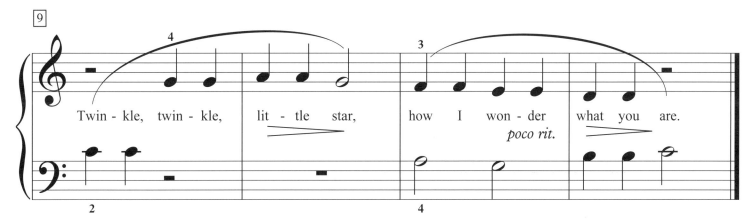

Optional Accompaniment (Student plays one octave higher than written.)

Moderately (♩ = 106)

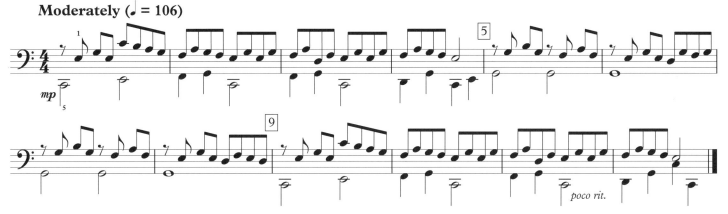

The Wheels on the Bus

Traditional
Arranged by Dennis Alexander

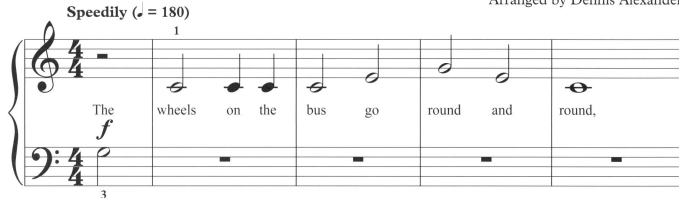

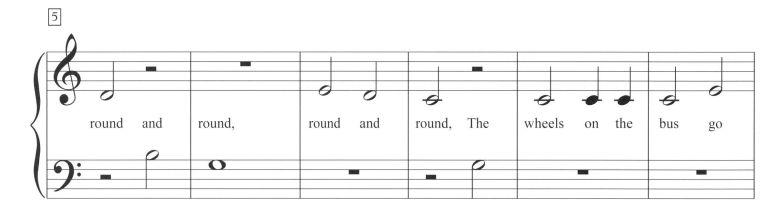

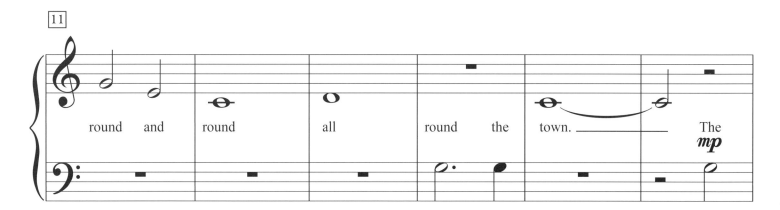

Optional Accompaniment (Student plays one octave higher than written.)

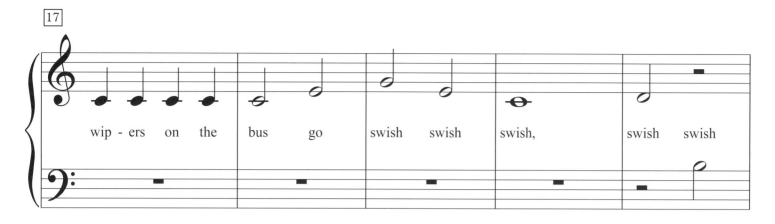

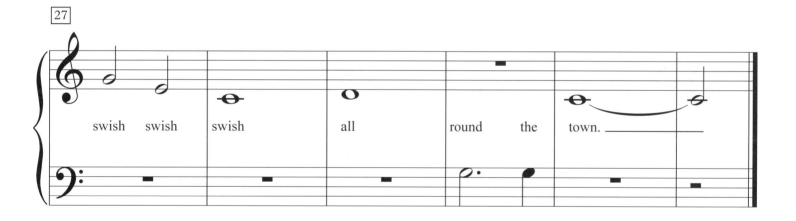

Pop Goes the Weasel

Traditional
Arranged by Dennis Alexander

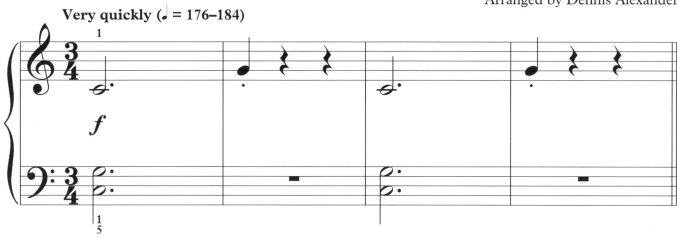

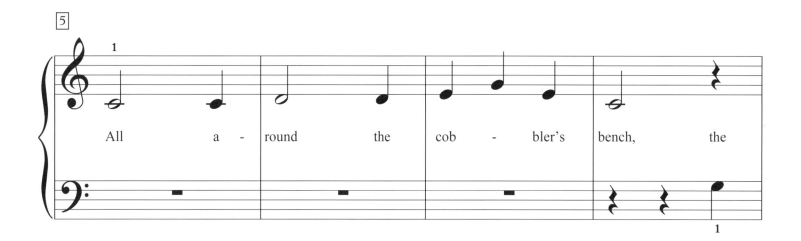

Optional Accompaniment (Student plays one octave higher than written.)

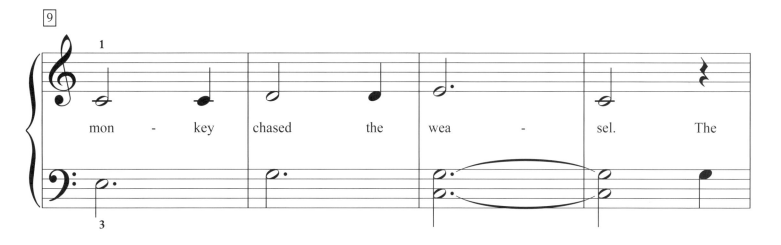

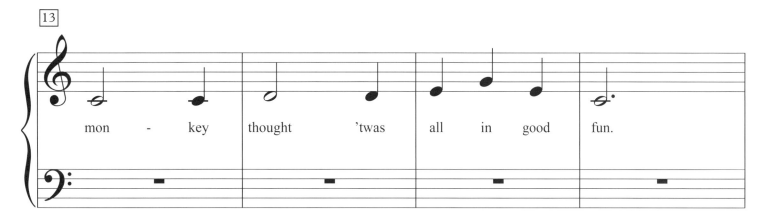

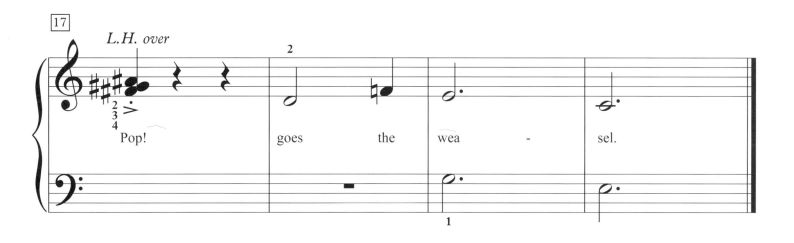

Old Joe Clark

Tennessee Folk Song
Arranged by Dennis Alexander

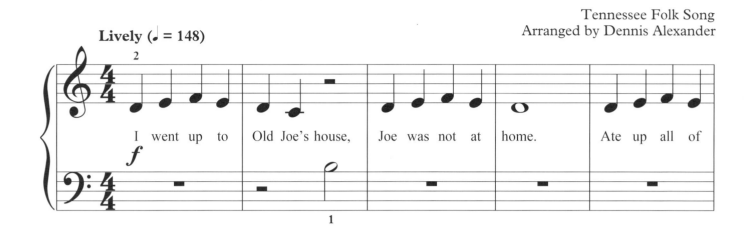

I went up to Old Joe's house, Joe was not at home. Ate up all of

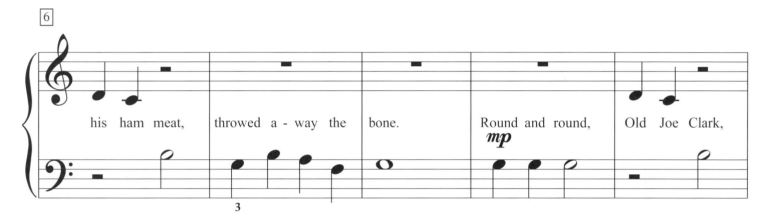

his ham meat, throwed a - way the bone. Round and round, Old Joe Clark,

Round and round I say, Round and round, Old Joe Clark, ain't got long to stay.

Optional Accompaniment (Student plays one octave higher than written.)

Hush, Little Baby

Carolina Folk Lullaby
Arranged by Dennis Alexander

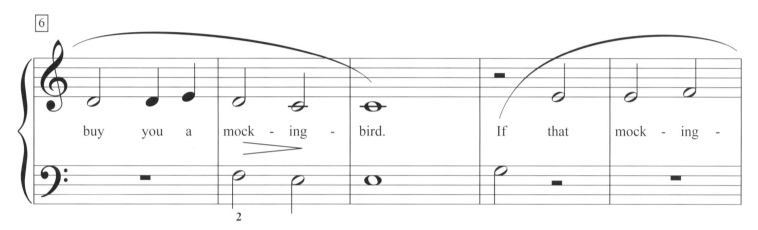

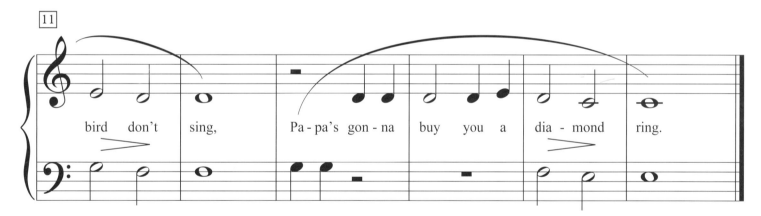

Optional Accompaniment (Student plays one octave higher than written.)

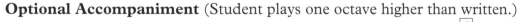

Go Tell Aunt Rhody

Traditional
Arranged by Dennis Alexander

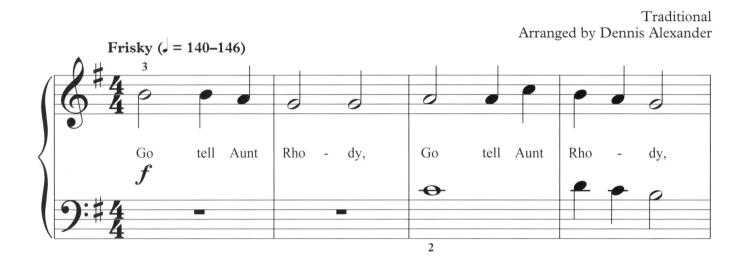

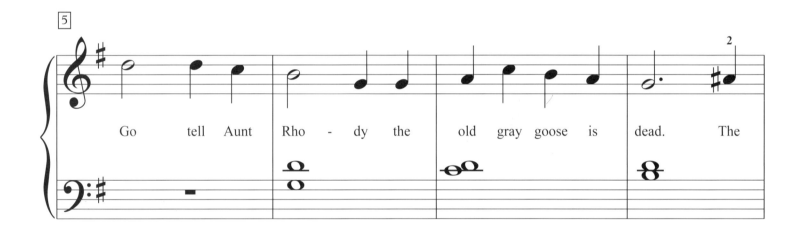

Optional Accompaniment (Student plays one octave higher than written.)

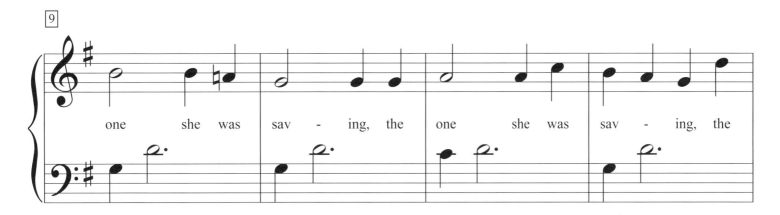

one   she   was   sav - ing, the   one   she   was   sav - ing, the

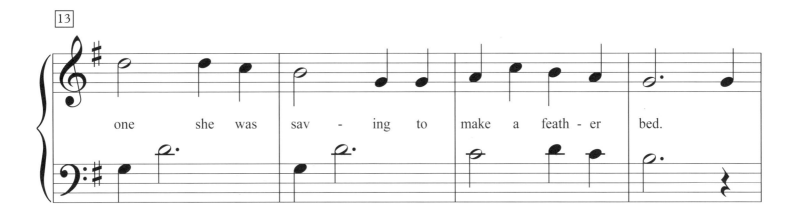

one   she   was   sav - ing   to   make   a   feath - er   bed.

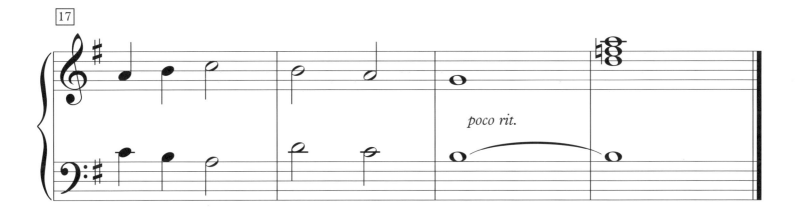

poco rit.

Hickory Dickory Dock

Traditional
Arranged by Dennis Alexander

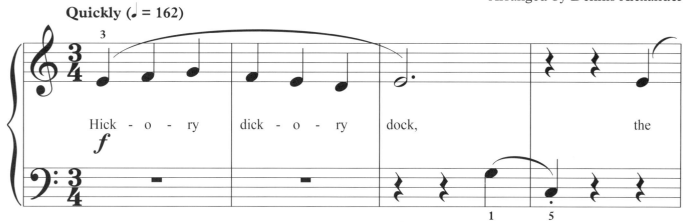

Hick - o - ry   dick - o - ry   dock,   the

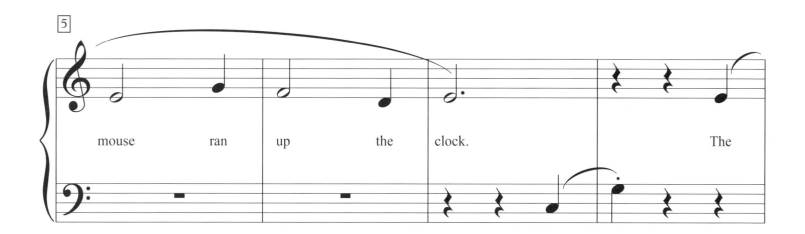

mouse   ran   up   the   clock.   The

Optional Accompaniment (Student plays one octave higher than written.)

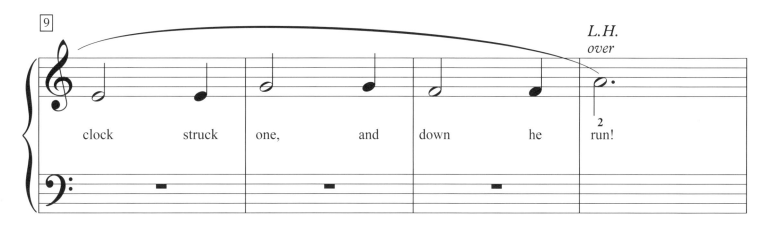

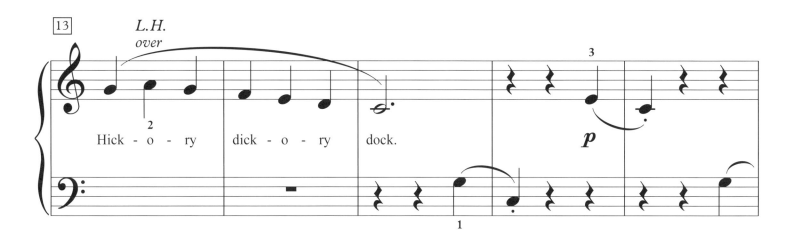

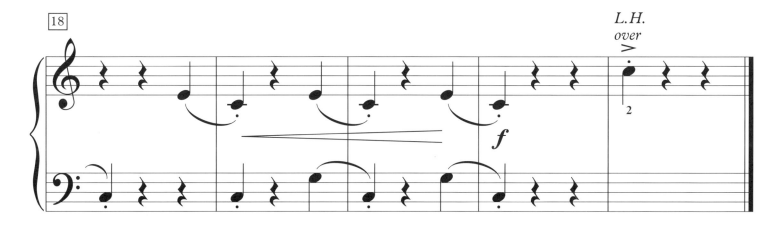

Here We Go Looby Loo

Traditional Folk Song
Arranged by Dennis Alexander

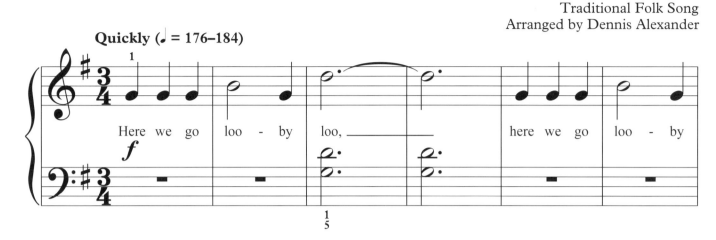

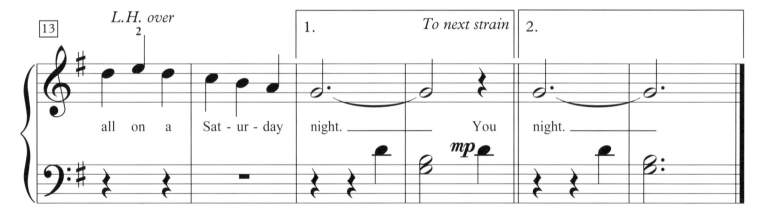

Optional Accompaniment (Student plays one octave higher than written.)

Quickly (♩ = 176–184)

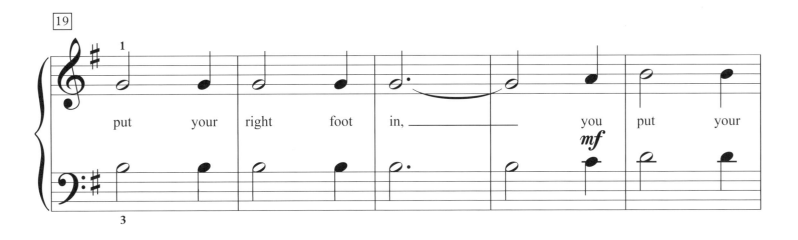

put your right foot in, _____ you put your

mf

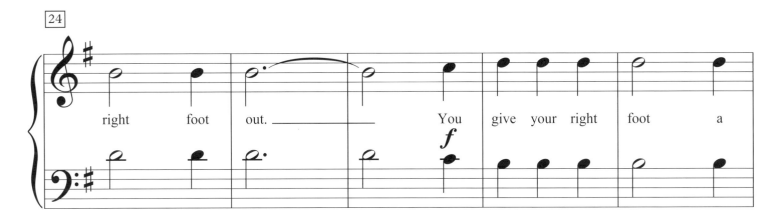

right foot out. _____ You give your right foot a

f

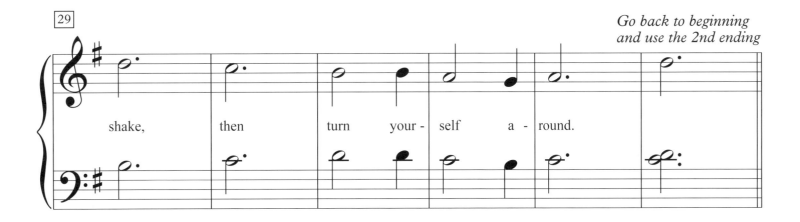

*Go back to beginning
and use the 2nd ending*

shake, then turn your-self a-round.

Oats, Peas, Beans, and Barley Grow

Traditional
Arranged by Dennis Alexander

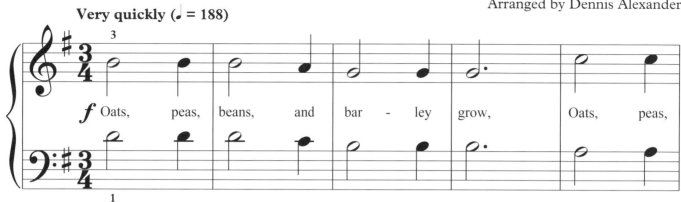

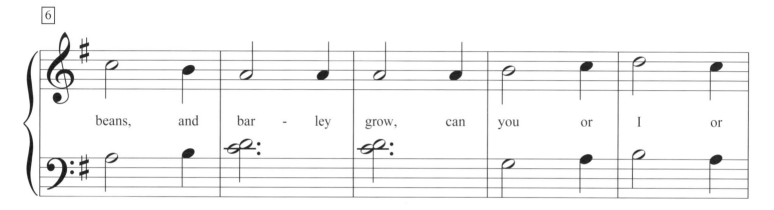

Optional Accompaniment (Student plays one octave higher than written.)

Very quickly (♩ = 188)

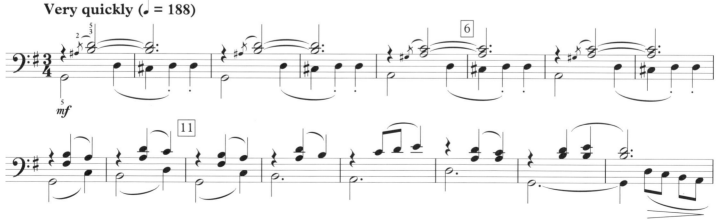

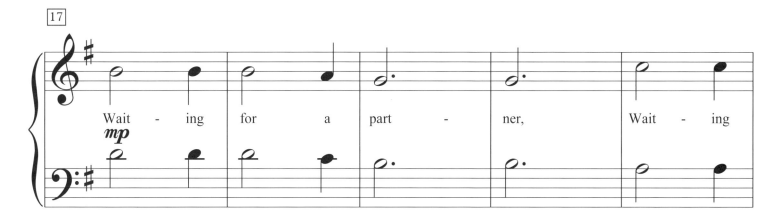

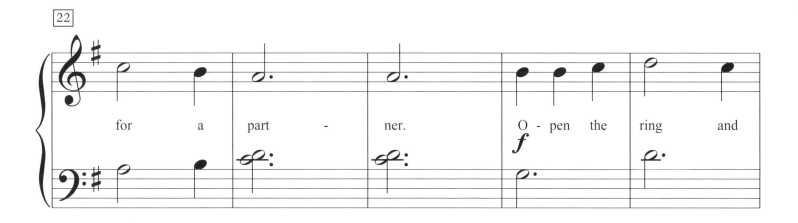

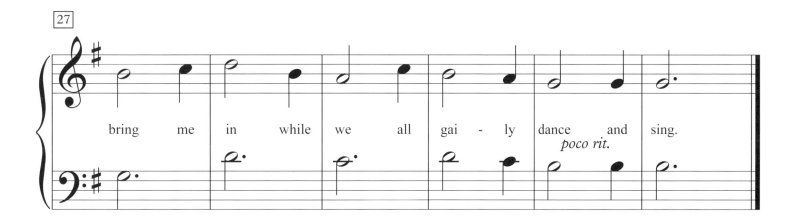

Lazy Mary, Will You Get Up?

Traditional
Arranged by Dennis Alexander

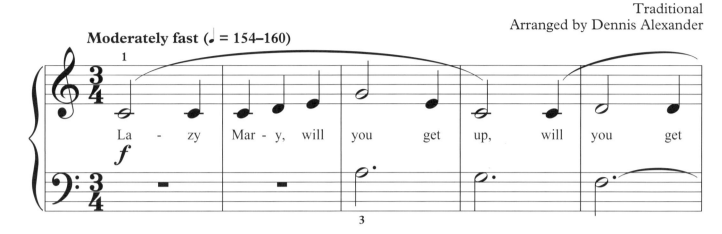

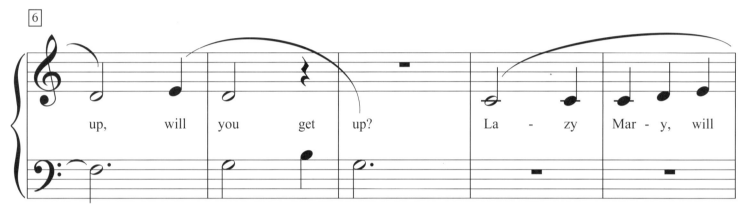

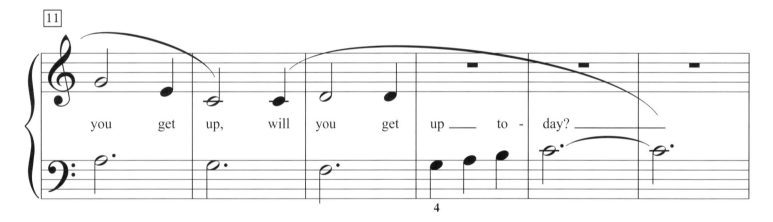

Optional Accompaniment (Student plays one octave higher than written.)

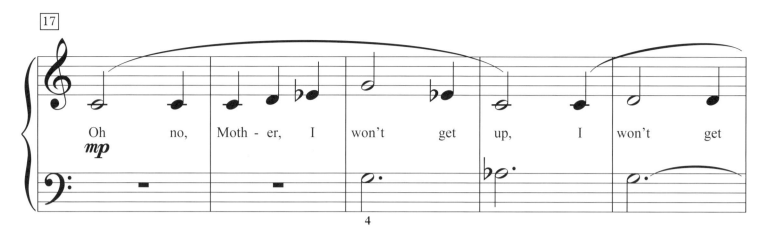

Oh no, Moth-er, I won't get up, I won't get

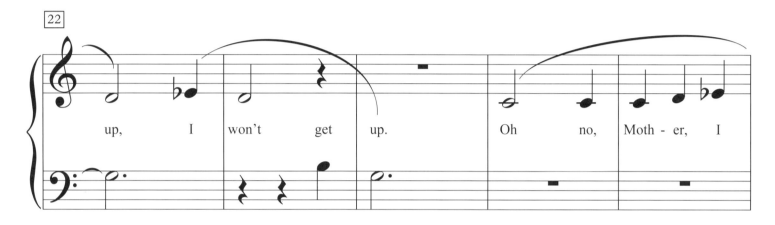

up, I won't get up. Oh no, Moth-er, I

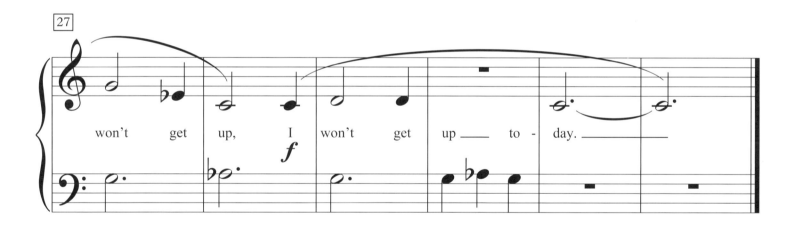

won't get up, I won't get up ___ to - day. ___

Alouette

Traditional
Arranged by Dennis Alexander

Moderately (♩ = 128–132)

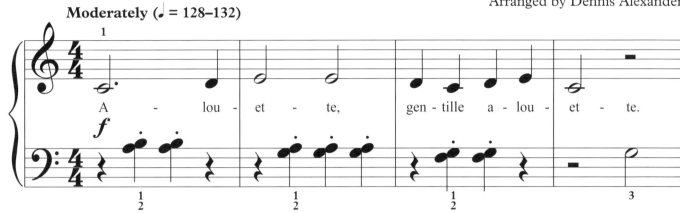

A - lou - et - te, gen - tille a - lou - et - te.

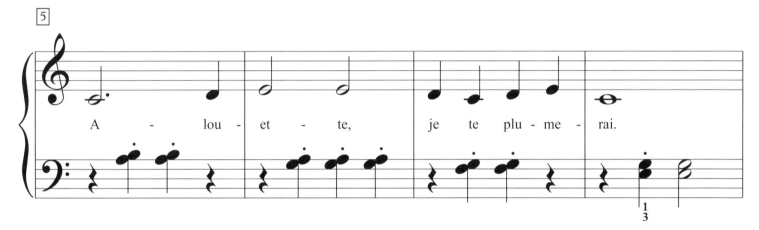

A - lou - et - te, je te plu - me - rai.

Je te plu - me - rai la tete, Je te plu - me - rai la tete.

Optional Accompaniment (Student plays one octave higher than written.)

Moderately (♩ = 128–132)

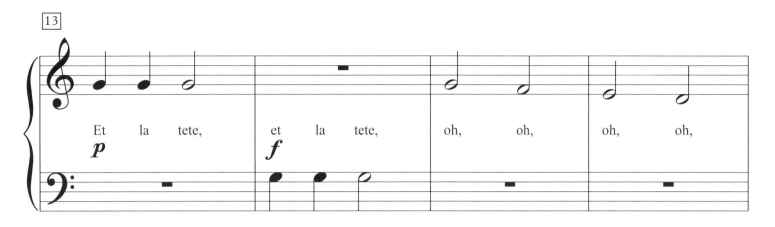

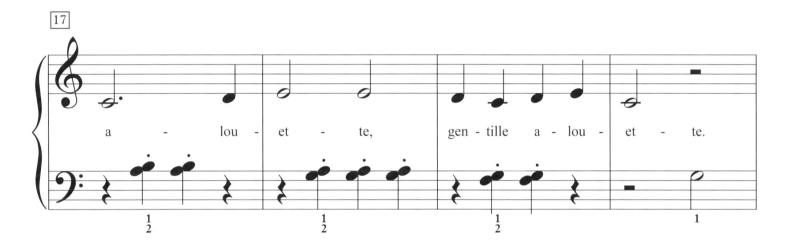

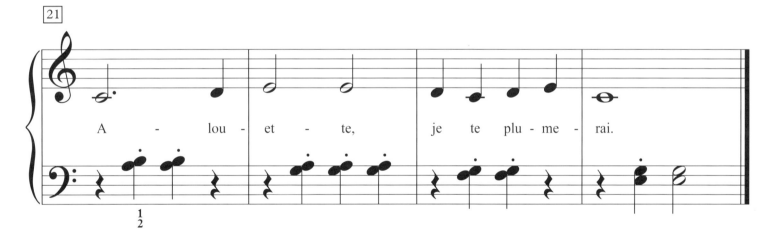

Eensy Weensy Spider

Traditional
Arranged by Dennis Alexander

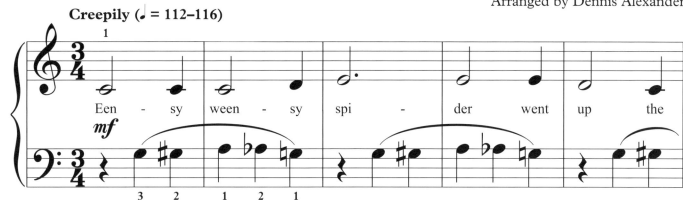

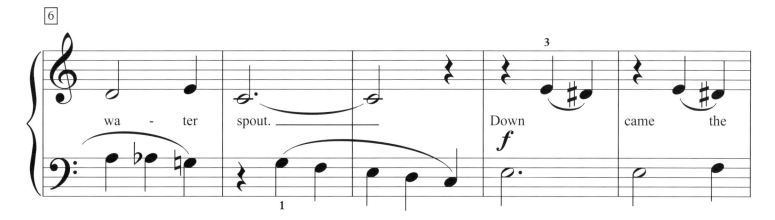

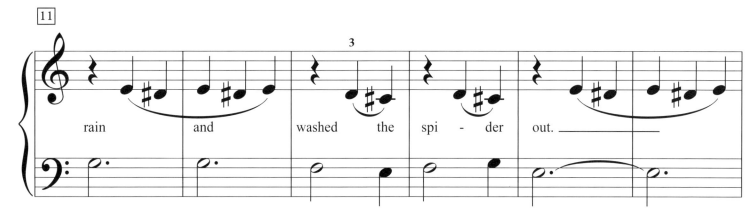

Optional Accompaniment (Student plays one octave higher than written.)

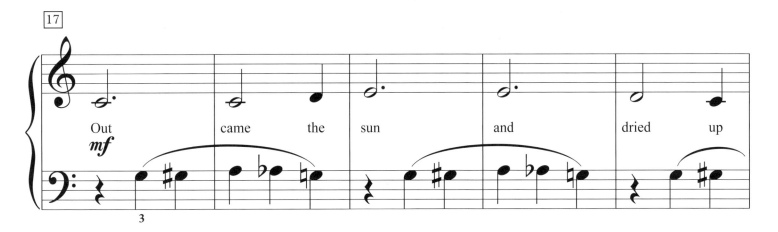

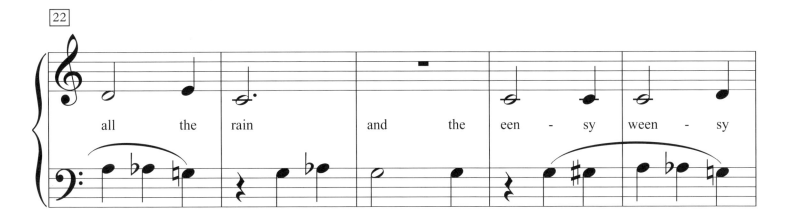

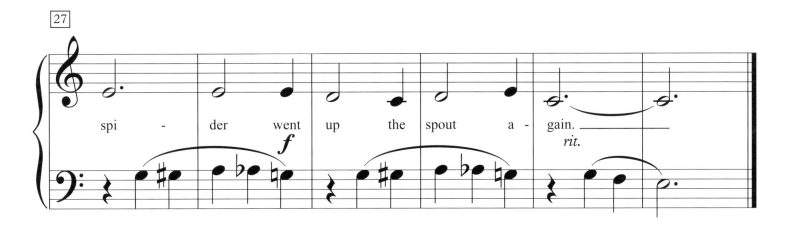

Sweetly Sings the Donkey

Traditional Round
Arranged by Dennis Alexander

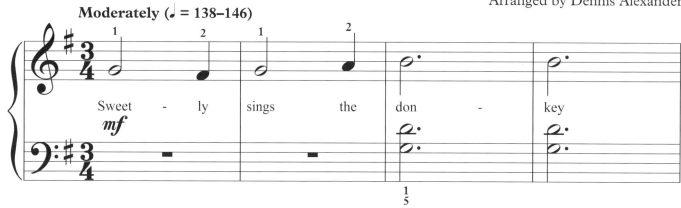

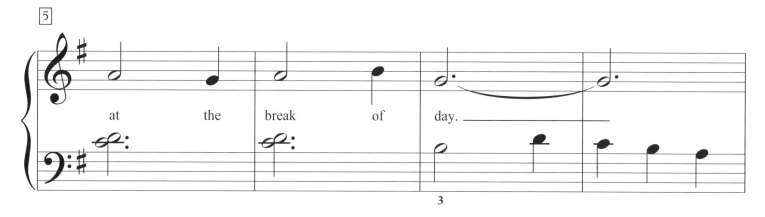

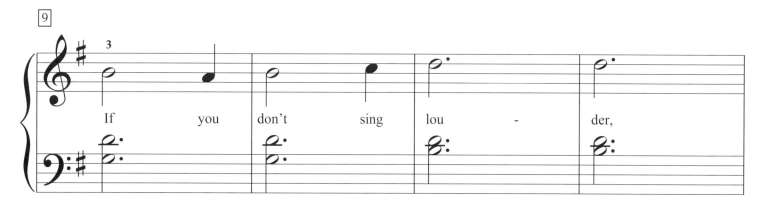

Optional Accompaniment (Student plays one octave higher than written.)

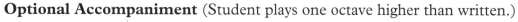

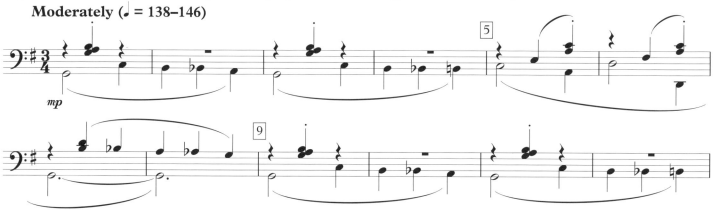

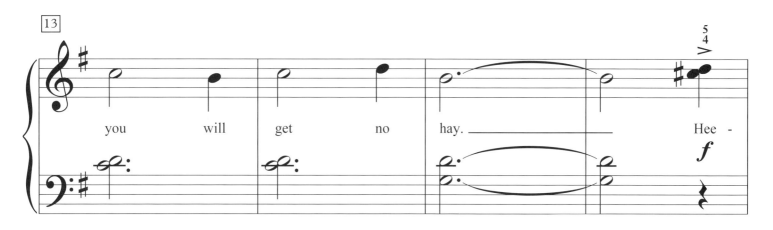

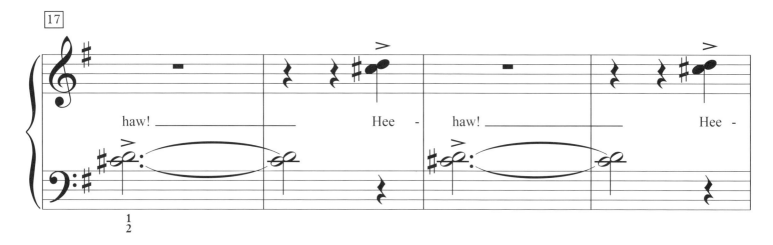

FOLK SONG COLLECTIONS
FOR PIANO

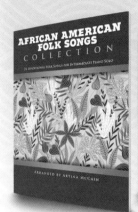

Introduce piano students to the music of world cultures with these folk songs arranged for intermediate piano solo. Each collection features 24 folk songs and includes detailed notes about the folk songs, beautiful illustrations, as well as a map of the regions.

AFRICAN AMERICAN FOLK SONGS COLLECTION
24 TRADITIONAL FOLK SONGS FOR
INTERMEDIATE LEVEL PIANO SOLO | *arr. Artina McCain*

The Bamboula • By and By • Deep River • Didn't My Lord Deliver Daniel? • Don't You Let Nobody Turn You Around • Every Time I Feel the Spirit • Give Me That Old Time Religion • Guide My Feet • I Want Jesus to Walk With Me • I Was Way Down A-Yonder • I'm a Soldier, Let Me Ride • In Bright Mansions Above • Lift Ev'ry Voice and Sing • Little David, Play on Your Harp • My Lord, What a Morning • Ride On, King Jesus • Run Mary Run • Sometimes I Feel Like a Motherless Child • Song of Conquest • Take Nabandji • Wade in the Water • Warriors' Song • Watch and Pray • What a Beautiful City.
00358084 Piano Solo...$12.99

IRISH FOLK SONGS COLLECTION
24 TRADITIONAL FOLK SONGS FOR
INTERMEDIATE LEVEL PIANO SOLO | *arr. June Armstrong*

As I Walked Out One Morning • Ballinderry • Blind Mary • Bunclody • Carrickfergus • The Castle of Dromore (The October Winds) • The Cliffs of Doneen • The Coolin • Courtin' in the Kitchen • Down Among the Ditches O • Down by the Salley Gardens • The Fairy Woman of Lough Leane • Follow Me Up to Carlow • The Gartan Mother's Lullaby • Huish the Cat • I'll Tell My Ma • Kitty of Coleraine • The Londonderry Air • My Lagan Love • My Love Is an Arbutus • Rocky Road to Dublin • Slieve Gallion Braes • Squire Parsons • That Night in Bethlehem.
00234359 Piano Solo.. $9.99

MALAY FOLK SONGS COLLECTION
24 TRADITIONAL SONGS ARRANGED FOR
INTERMEDIATE LEVEL PIANO SOLO | *arr. Charmaine Siagian*

At Dawn • Chan Mali Chan • C'mon, Mama! • The Cockatoo • The Curvy Water Spinach Stalk • Five Little Chicks • God Bless the Sultan • The Goodbye Song • Great Indonesia • It's All Good Here • The Jumping Frog • Longing • Mak Inang • Milk Coffee • The Moon Kite • Morning Tide • My Country • Onward Singapore • Ponyfish • Song for the Ladybugs • The Stork Song • Suriram • Trek Tek Tek • Voyage of the Sampan.
00288420 Piano Solo.. $10.99

CHINESE FOLK SONGS COLLECTION
24 TRADITIONAL SONGS ARRANGED FOR
INTERMEDIATE LEVEL PIANO SOLO | *arr. Joseph Johnson*

Beating the Wild Hog • Blue Flower • Carrying Song • Crescent Moon • Darkening Sky • Digging for Potatoes • Girl's Lament • Great Wall • Hand Drum Song • Homesick • Jasmine Flower Song • Little Cowherd • Love Song of the Prarie • Memorial • Mountaintop View • Northwest Rains • Running Horse Mountain • Sad, Rainy Day • Song of the Clown • The Sun Came Up Happy • Wa-Ha-Ha • Wedding Veil • White Flower • Woven Basket.
00296764 Piano Solo $10.99

KOREAN FOLK SONGS COLLECTION
24 TRADITIONAL FOLK SONGS FOR
INTERMEDIATE LEVEL PIANO SOLO | *arr. Lawrence Lee*

Arirang • Autumn in the City • Birdie, Birdie • Boat Song • Catch the Tail • Chestnut • Cricket • Dance in the Moonlight • Five Hundred Years • Flowers • Fun Is Here • The Gate • Han River • Harvest • Jindo Field Song • Lullaby • The Mill • The Palace • The Pier • Three-Way Junction • Waterfall • Wild Herbs • Yearning • You and I.
00296810 Piano Solo.. $10.99

JAPANESE FOLK SONGS COLLECTION
24 TRADITIONAL FOLK SONGS FOR
INTERMEDIATE LEVEL PIANO SOLO | *arr. Mika Goto*

Blooming Flowers • Come Here, Fireflies • Counting Game • The Fisherman's Song • Going to the Shrine • Harvest Song • Itsuki Lullaby • Joyful Doll Festival • Kimigayo • Let's Sing • My Hometown • Picking Tea Leaves • The Rabbit on the Moon • Rain • Rain Showers • Rock-Paper-Scissors • Sakura • Seven Baby Crows • Takeda Lullaby • Time to Go Home • Village Festival • Where Are You From? • Wish I Could Go • You're It!
00296891 Piano Solo.. $9.99

HAL•LEONARD®

halleonard.com

Prices, contents and availability subject to change without notice.

This series showcases great original piano music from our **Hal Leonard Student Piano Library** family of composers. Carefully graded for easy selection.

BILL BOYD

JAZZ BITS (AND PIECES)
Early Intermediate Level
00290312 11 Solos......................$7.99

JAZZ DELIGHTS
Intermediate Level
00240435 11 Solos......................$8.99

JAZZ FEST
Intermediate Level
00240436 10 Solos......................$8.99

JAZZ PRELIMS
Early Elementary Level
00290032 12 Solos......................$7.99

JAZZ SKETCHES
Intermediate Level
00220001 8 Solos......................$8.99

JAZZ STARTERS
Elementary Level
00290425 10 Solos......................$8.99

JAZZ STARTERS II
Late Elementary Level
00290434 11 Solos......................$7.99

JAZZ STARTERS III
Late Elementary Level
00290465 12 Solos......................$8.99

THINK JAZZ!
Early Intermediate Level
00290417 Method Book............$12.99

TONY CARAMIA

JAZZ MOODS
Intermediate Level
00296728 8 Solos......................$6.95

SUITE DREAMS
Intermediate Level
00296775 4 Solos......................$6.99

SONDRA CLARK

DAKOTA DAYS
Intermediate Level
00296521 5 Solos......................$6.95

FLORIDA FANTASY SUITE
Intermediate Level
00296766 3 Duets......................$7.95

THREE ODD METERS
Intermediate Level
00296472 3 Duets......................$6.95

MATTHEW EDWARDS

CONCERTO FOR YOUNG PIANISTS
FOR 2 PIANOS, FOUR HANDS
Intermediate Level Book/CD
00296356 3 Movements $19.99

CONCERTO NO. 2 IN G MAJOR
FOR 2 PIANOS, 4 HANDS
Intermediate Level Book/CD
00296670 3 Movements............$17.99

PHILLIP KEVEREN

MOUSE ON A MIRROR
Late Elementary Level
00296361 5 Solos......................$8.99

MUSICAL MOODS
Elementary/Late Elementary Level
00296714 7 Solos......................$6.99

SHIFTY-EYED BLUES
Late Elementary Level
00296374 5 Solos......................$7.99

CAROL KLOSE

THE BEST OF CAROL KLOSE
Early to Late Intermediate Level
00146151 15 Solos....................$12.99

CORAL REEF SUITE
Late Elementary Level
00296354 7 Solos......................$7.50

DESERT SUITE
Intermediate Level
00296667 6 Solos......................$7.99

FANCIFUL WALTZES
Early Intermediate Level
00296473 5 Solos......................$7.95

GARDEN TREASURES
Late Intermediate Level
00296787 5 Solos......................$8.50

ROMANTIC EXPRESSIONS
Intermediate to Late Intermediate Level
00296923 5 Solos......................$8.99

WATERCOLOR MINIATURES
Early Intermediate Level
00296848 7 Solos......................$7.99

JENNIFER LINN

AMERICAN IMPRESSIONS
Intermediate Level
00296471 6 Solos......................$8.99

ANIMALS HAVE FEELINGS TOO
Early Elementary/Elementary Level
00147789 8 Solos......................$8.99

AU CHOCOLAT
Late Elementary/Early Intermediate Level
00298110 7 Solos......................$8.99

CHRISTMAS IMPRESSIONS
Intermediate Level
00296706 8 Solos......................$8.99

JUST PINK
Elementary Level
00296722 9 Solos......................$8.99

LES PETITES IMAGES
Late Elementary Level
00296664 7 Solos......................$8.99

LES PETITES IMPRESSIONS
Intermediate Level
00296355 6 Solos......................$8.99

REFLECTIONS
Late Intermediate Level
00296843 5 Solos......................$8.99

TALES OF MYSTERY
Intermediate Level
00296769 6 Solos......................$8.99

LYNDA LYBECK-ROBINSON

ALASKA SKETCHES
Early Intermediate Level
00119637 8 Solos......................$8.99

AN AWESOME ADVENTURE
Late Elementary Level
00137563 8 Solos......................$7.99

FOR THE BIRDS
Early Intermediate/Intermediate Level
00237078 9 Solos......................$8.99

WHISPERING WOODS
Late Elementary Level
00275905 9 Solos......................$8.99

MONA REJINO

CIRCUS SUITE
Late Elementary Level
00296665 5 Solos......................$8.99

COLOR WHEEL
Early Intermediate Level
00201951 6 Solos......................$9.99

IMPRESIONES DE ESPAÑA
Intermediate Level
00337520 6 Solos......................$8.99

IMPRESSIONS OF NEW YORK
Intermediate Level
00364212................................$8.99

JUST FOR KIDS
Elementary Level
00296840 8 Solos......................$7.99

MERRY CHRISTMAS MEDLEYS
Intermediate Level
00296799 5 Solos......................$8.99

MINIATURES IN STYLE
Intermediate Level
00148088 6 Solos......................$8.99

PORTRAITS IN STYLE
Early Intermediate Level
00296507 6 Solos......................$8.99

EUGÉNIE ROCHEROLLE

CELEBRATION SUITE
Intermediate Level
00152724 3 Duets......................$8.99

ENCANTOS ESPAÑOLES (SPANISH DELIGHTS)
Intermediate Level
00125451 6 Solos......................$8.99

JAMBALAYA
Intermediate Level
00296654 2 Pianos, 8 Hands.....$12.99
00296725 2 Pianos, 4 Hands.......$7.95

JEROME KERN CLASSICS
Intermediate Level
00296577 10 Solos....................$12.99

LITTLE BLUES CONCERTO
Early Intermediate Level
00142801 2 Pianos, 4 Hands......$12.99

TOUR FOR TWO
Late Elementary Level
00296832 6 Duets......................$9.99

TREASURES
Late Elementary/Early Intermediate Level
00296924 7 Solos......................$8.99

JEREMY SISKIND

BIG APPLE JAZZ
Intermediate Level
00278209 8 Solos......................$8.99

MYTHS AND MONSTERS
Late Elementary/Early Intermediate Level
00148148 9 Solos......................$8.99

CHRISTOS TSITSAROS

DANCES FROM AROUND THE WORLD
Early Intermediate Level
00296688 7 Solos......................$8.99

FIVE SUMMER PIECES
Late Intermediate/Advanced Level
00361235 5 Solos....................$12.99

LYRIC BALLADS
Intermediate/Late Intermediate Level
00102404 6 Solos......................$8.99

POETIC MOMENTS
Intermediate Level
00296403 8 Solos......................$8.99

SEA DIARY
Early Intermediate Level
00253486 9 Solos......................$8.99

SONATINA HUMORESQUE
Late Intermediate Level
00296772 3 Movements..............$6.99

SONGS WITHOUT WORDS
Intermediate Level
00296506 9 Solos......................$9.99

THREE PRELUDES
Early Advanced Level
00130747 3 Solos......................$8.99

THROUGHOUT THE YEAR
Late Elementary Level
00296723 12 Duets....................$6.95

ADDITIONAL COLLECTIONS

AT THE LAKE
by Elvina Pearce
Elementary/Late Elementary Level
00131642 10 Solos and Duets.....$7.99

CHRISTMAS FOR TWO
by Dan Fox
Early Intermediate Level
00290069 13 Duets....................$8.99

CHRISTMAS JAZZ
by Mike Springer
Intermediate Level
00296525 6 Solos......................$8.99

COUNTY RAGTIME FESTIVAL
by Fred Kern
Intermediate Level
00296882 7 Solos......................$7.99

LITTLE JAZZERS
by Jennifer Watts
Elementary/Late Elementary Level
00154573 9 Solos......................$8.99

PLAY THE BLUES!
by Luann Carman
Early Intermediate Level
00296357 10 Solos....................$9.99

ROLLER COASTERS & RIDES
by Jennifer & Mike Watts
Intermediate Level
00131144 8 Duets......................$8.99

www.halleonard.com

DENNIS ALEXANDER has earned an international reputation as one of North America's most prolific and popular composers of educational piano music. In 2015, he was honored by the National Conference on Keyboard Pedagogy with the Lifetime Achievement Award, and his two Nocturnes collections received the prestigious MTNA/Frances Clark Pedagogy Award in 2020. His compositions are routinely included in the National Federation of Music bulletin, and his music is performed by students in the United States and around the world.

Mr. Alexander is a native Kansan and graduate of the University of Kansas. From 1972 to 1996, he was on the faculty of the University of Montana and served as department chair in addition to teaching duties in applied piano, class piano, and piano pedagogy. After retiring, he served on the faculties of Cal State Fullerton and Cal State Northridge. He has toured worldwide, performing recitals and presenting workshops in Hong Kong, India, Indonesia, Malaysia, Singapore, and South Korea.

Mr. Alexander currently lives in Albuquerque, New Mexico where he continues an active composing and touring schedule. For more information, **visit www.DennisAlexander.com**, which features recordings, videos, teaching tips, and more.